Anonymous

Road Overseer's Commission

With road law

Anonymous

Road Overseer's Commission
With road law

ISBN/EAN: 9783337421342

Printed in Europe, USA, Canada, Australia, Japan

Cover: Foto ©Suzi / pixelio.de

More available books at **www.hansebooks.com**

Road Precinct No.

FROM

....

....

TO **Road Overseer's Commission**

... WITH ROAD LAW ...

....

.... **ROAD OVERSEER.**

ISSUED .... *day of*....... ...189........

~
......*Term,* 189........

COMMISSIONERS' COURT,

.... *County,*

TEXAS.

.... **COUNTY CLERK.**

By ....

DEPUTY.

THE STATE OF TEXAS, } IN THE COMMISSIONERS' COURT,

Term, A. D. 189 ——

County of ————————

IT IS ORDERED BY THE COURT, That ———————— be appointed to serve until the first regular meeting of said Court, of the year 189 ——, or until the appoint- ment of his successor, as Overseer of the ———————— which is bounded as follows, to-wit:

Road Precinct No.

and includes all the Public Roads within the aforesaid boundaries.

AND IT IS FURTHER ORDERED, That he have the following named hands to work said road, to-wit:

....

....

....

....

with authority to summon any and all other persons, not designated herein, and known to him to be liable

to work on the Public Roads within said Precinct.

    I HEREBY CERTIFY That the above is a true and correct copy from the

      Minutes of said Court at said Term.

    Given under my hand and seal of said Court, this ....*day of*

.... *A. D. 189*

.... *County Clerk.*

By .... *Deputy.*

ARTICLE 4359. All public roads and highways that have heretofore been laid out and established agreeably to law, except such as have been discontinued, are hereby declared to be public roads.

What roads are public.

ART. 4360. The commissioners' courts of the several counties shall have full power, and it shall be their duty to order the laying-out and opening of public roads when necessary, and to discontinue or alter any road whenever it shall be deemed expedient, as hereinafter prescribed. *Provided*, that hereafter no public road shall be altered or changed, except for the purpose of shortening the distance from the point of beginning to the point of destination, unless the court upon a full investigation of the proposed change find that the public interest will be better served by making the change. That said change shall be by unanimous consent of all the commissioners elected.

Power of com- m'rs' court to open.

Can be altered only to shorten unless,&c.

(Acts '89 P. 21.)

ART. 4361. It shall be the duty of the commissioners' courts to classify all public roads in their counties into first, second and third class roads, and to act as supervisors of roads in their respective precincts as hereinafter provided, and commissioners' courts may, on their own motion, where it is deemed necessary, open new roads or straighten existing ones.

Roads shall be classified.

(Acts '84 P. 21)

ART. 4362. First-class roads shall be clear of all obstructions, and not less than forty feet nor more than sixty feet wide; all stumps over six inches in diameter to be cut down to six inches of the surface and rounded off; all stumps six inches and under to be cut smooth with the ground, and all causeways made at least sixteen feet wide.

1st-class Road.

ART. 4363. Second-class roads shall be clear of all obstructions and not less than thirty-   feet wide; stumps six inches and over in diameter to be cut down to six inches of the surface and rounded off; and all stumps less than six inches in diameter to be cut smooth with the ground; all causeways to be made at least sixteen feet wide.

2d-class Road.

ART. 4364. Third-class roads shall be clear of all obstructions, and not less than twenty feet wide; stumps six inches and over in diameter to be cut down to six inches of the surface and rounded off; all stumps less than six inches in diameter to be cut smooth with the ground, and all causeways made at least twelve feet wide.

3d-class Road.

ART. 4365. The commissioners' court shall in no instance grant an order on application for any new road, or to discontinue an original one, unless the persons making application therefor, or some one of them, shall have given at least twenty days' notice by written advertisement of their intended application, posted up at the court house door of the county, and at two other public public places in the vicinity of the route of the proposed new road, or the road proposed to be discontinued.

Order for new Road, Etc, granted only after due notice.

ART. 4366. All applications for a new road, and all applications to discontinue an existing one, shall be by petition to the commissioners' court, signed by at least eight freeholders in the precinct or precincts in which such road is desired to be made or discontinued, specifying in such petition the beginning and termination of such road proposed to be opened or discontinued; *provided*, that where one or more persons live within any

Requisites of application.

enclosure, either or all of them may petition the commissioners' court for a third-class road or neighborhood road to their nearest trading points, mills, gins, school and church houses and county seats, and the courts shall open such roads, as hereinafter provided in the opening of third class roads; and *provided further*, that

no part of a public road shall be discontinued, unless a new road connecting that part of such road not discontinued, shall first be opened; and *provided further*, that no part of a first or second class road shall be reduced to a road of a lower class.

Jury of freeholders with or without Co. Surveyor to lay out Road.

(Acts '85 P. 92)

ART. 4367. All roads hereafter ordered to be made shall be laid out by a jury of freeholders of the county, to be appointed by the commissioners' court. Said jury shall consist of five persons, a majority of whom may proceed, with or without the county surveyor as ordered by the commissioners' court, to lay out, survey and describe such road, to the greatest advantage to the public, and so that the same can be traced with certainty, and the field notes of such survey or description of the road shall be included in the report of the jury, and if adopted shall be recorded in the minutes of the commissioners' court.

ART. 4368. The jurors provided for in the preceding article shall, before proceeding to act as such, take the following oath before some officer authorized to administer oaths, to-wit:

"I,.............., do solemnly swear that I will lay out the road now directed to be laid out by the order to us directed from the commissioners' court, according to law, without favor or affection, malice or hatred, to the best of my skill and knowledge, so help me God."

ART. 4369. It shall be the duty of such jurors, when qualified as provided in the preceding article, to proceed to lay out and mark the road in accordance with the order of the court and the law, and to report their proceedings in writing to the next regular term of the commissioners' court.

ART. 4370. The jury of freeholders provided for in article 4367 shall issue a notice in writing to the land owners through whose land the proposed road may run, or to his agent or attorney, of the time when they will proceed to lay out such road, or when they will assess the damages incidental to the opening of the same, which notice shall be served upon such owner, his agent or attorney, at least five days before the day therein named. If such owner is a non-resident of the county, the notice may be given by publication in a newspaper published in the county, as notices are required to be given to non-resident defendants as to action in the district or county court, and the road may be established after four weeks' publication, the cost of publication to be paid as directed by judgment of the court.

ART. 4371. The owner of any such land may, at the time stated in such notice, or previously thereto, present to the jury a statement in writing of the damages claimed by him, if any, incidental to the opening of such road, and thereupon the jury shall proceed to assess the damages, returning their assessment and the claimant's statement with their report to the commissioners' court.

ART. 4372. If the commissioners' court shall approve of the report and order such road to be opened, they shall consider the assessment of damages by the jury and the claimant's statement thereof, and allow to such owner just damages and adequate compensation for the land taken, and when paid or secured by deposit with the county treasurer, to the credit of such owner, they may proceed to have such road opened. If the owner of the land is not satisfied with the assessment by the commissioners' court, he may appeal therefrom as in cases of appeal from judgment of justice's court, but such appeal shall not prevent the road from being opened, but shall be only to fix the amount of damages. If no claim of damages is filed with such jury, after notice as provided in the preceding article, the same shall be considered as waived.

Owner may appeal.

If no claim filed dam'ges considered waived.

(Acts '84 P. 22)

ART. 4373. If, in the judgment of the commissioners' court, from the report of the commissioner named in the two preceding articles, the road should be deemed of sufficient importance, the court may order the survey or opening of the same; but the court shall first order the payment of the damages assessed, if any, by the commissioners of view to be made to the owners of the land out of the county treasury, and the county treasurer shall have paid the same or secured its payment by special deposit of the amount in his office, subject to the order of such owner, and shall notify such owner by mail or otherwise of such deposit.

Road may be opened but dam'es must first be paid.

ART. 4374. If no objection be filed, upon the report of a jury appointed upon an application to open a new road, the court shall proceed to establish and classify such road, and classify such road, and order the opening out of the same, and shall appoint an overseer and apportion hands for the same, as in other cases.

Road established.

ART. 4375. The commissioners' court may alter or change the course of any public road in accordance with article 4360 of this chapter, after notice and upon application in the same manner as provided in this chapter for the discontinuance of a road, except that the application need not be signed by more than one freeholder of the precinct in which such alteration or change is proposed to be made.

Roads may be altered.

(Acts '84 P. 22)

ART. 4376. When juries of view are appointed, it shall be the duty of the clerk of the court to make out copies of the order appointing them in duplicate, and to deliver such copies to the sheriff of the county within ten days after such order of appointment was made, endorsing on such copies the date of such order.

Duty of Clerk, when jury of view is appointed.

ART. 4377. The sheriff receiving such copies shall serve the same upon the jurors by delivering to each of them in person a copy of the order of appointment provided for in the preceding article, or by leaving one of said copies at the usual place of abode of such juror. Service shall be made within twenty days after the sheriff receives said copies, and he shall make his return to the clerk on the duplicate copies, stating the date and manner of service, or if service has not been made, stating the cause of his failure to make the same.

Sheriff to serve notice on jurors.

ART. 4378. Any juror of view, summoned as such, who shall fail or refuse to perform the service required of him by law as such juror, shall forfeit and pay for every such failure the sum of ten dollars, to be recovered by judgment on motion of the district or county attorney, in the name of the county, in any court of competent jurisdiction of the county in which such defaulter may reside.

Juror shall forfeit $10 00 for failure to serve.

ART. 4379. For the further and better providing for public roads, any lines between different persons or owners of land, any section line, or any direct line through an enclosure containing twelve hundred and

Certain lines bet'n owners may be declared highways.

(Acts '84 P. 22) eighty acres of land or more, may, upon the conditions provided for in the following articles of this chapter. be declared public highways, and left open and free from obstructions for fifteen feet on either side of said lines, but the marked trees and other objects used to designate said lines, and the corners of surveys, shall not be removed or defaced.

Manner of securing neighbor-hood Roads.
ART. 4380. Whenever ten freeholders may desire the boundary lines between different persons or owners of land to be declared a public highway, in order to give them a nearer, better or more practicable road to their church, county seat, mill, timber or water, they may apply to the commissioners' court for an order establishing such road.

Applicat'n, its requisites.
ART. 4381. The application provided for in the preceding article shall be in writing, and shall be signed and sworn to by the applicants. It shall designate the lines sought to be opened and the names and residences of the persons or owners to be affected by such proposed road, and shall state the facts which show a necessity for such road.

Clerk shall issue notice.
ART. 4382. Upon the filing of such application, the clerk shall issue a notice reciting the substance thereof, directed to the sheriff or any constable of the county, commanding him to summon the owners of the land, naming them, whose lines are proposed to be left open, to appear at the next regular term of the commissioners' court to show cause why said lands should not be declared public highways.

Service of no-tice and re-turn.
ART. 4383. The notice provided for in the preceding article shall be served in the manner and for the length of time provided for the service of citations in civil actions in justices' courts, and shall be returned in like manner as such citations.

County Com'rs may declare the lines a highway.

(Acts '84 P. 23)
ART. 4384. At a regular term of the court, after due service of notice as provided in the preceding article. the commissioners' court may, in its discretion, should it deem the road of sufficient public importance, issue an order declaring the lines designated in the application to be public highways, and direct that the same be opened by the owners thereof, and left open for a space of fifteen feet on each side of said line.

Notice shall be served upon owners.
ART. 4385. When an order as provided in the preceding article is made, the clerk shall without delay issue a notice reciting said order or its substance, directed to the sheriff or any constable of the county, commanding him to serve the owners of such lines named in such notice with a true copy thereof, and the officer to whom said notice is delivered shall without delay serve the same as therein directed, and return the same to the clerk, endorsing thereon the manner and date of such service.

Shall not be worked by Road hands.
ART. 4386. The commissioners' court shall not be required to keep any such road as is mentioned in the last seven articles worked by road hands, as is the case with other public roads.

Cost of open-ing neigh-borhood Roads to be paid by Co. (Acts '84 P. 23)
ART. 4387. All costs attending the proceedings provided for in relation to opening of neighborhood roads shall be paid for by the county, if the application be granted.

Shall be dis-continued as other public Roads.
ART. 4388. The commissioners' court may discontinue any neighborhood road which has been established as a public highway, in the same manner provided in this chapter for discontinuing other public roads

ART. 4389. The owners of the land whose lines have been or may be declared public highways, and also any person through whose land a third class road may run, shall have the right to erect a gate or gates across said road or roads when necessary, said gate or gates to be not less than ten feet wide and free of obstructions at the top; *provided*, that when the right of way for any third class road or neighborhood road has been granted to the county without cost, the owner of such land shall have the right to put a gate across such road or roads; but where such right of way has been condemned and paid for according to existing law. the county commissioners' court shall have the right to prevent any obstruction of such a road by a gate.

Gates may be erected across certain Roads.

(Acts '84 P. 23)

ART. 4390. The amount of damages to be allowed to the owners of said lands for opening the line of a neighborhood road, as provided in this chapter, shall be assessed as provided for in the case of first, second and third class roads in this chapter.

Damages in opening 3rd class Roads.

(Acts '84 P. 23)

ART. 4390a. The county commissioners of the several counties are hereby constituted supervisors of public roads in their respective counties, and each commissioner shall supervise the public roads within his commissioners' precinct once each year, and shall receive as compensation therefor three dollars per day for the time actually employed in the discharge of his duties, to be paid out of the road and bridge fund of the county; *provided*, that no commissioner shall receive pay for more than ten days in each year. He shall also make a report to the first regular term of the commissioners' court held in this county during the year, said report to be made under oath, and to state: First, the condition of all roads and parts of roads in his precinct. Second, the condition of all culverts and bridges. Third, the amount of money remaining in the hands of overseers subject to be expended upon the roads within his precinct. Fourth, the number of mile posts and finger boards defaced and torn down. Fifth, what, if any, new roads of any kind should be opened in his precinct, and what, if any, bridges, culverts or other improvements are necessary to place the roads in his precinct in good condition and the probable cost of such improvements; also the name of any overseer who has failed to work the road, or in any way neglected to perform his duty. Said report shall be spread upon the minutes of the court to be considered in improving public roads and determining the amount of taxes to be levied therefor, and if any commissioner of any commissioners' court in any county in this State shall fail or refuse to discharge any or all duties made obligatory upon him by the provisions of section 1, article 4390a, he shall be deemed guilty of a misdemeanor, and, upon conviction therefor before any court of competent jurisdiction, shall be fined in any sum not less than ten nor more than fifty dollars.

Co. Comm'ers made supervisors of Roads.

His annual report.

Report spread on minutes.

Penalty.

(Acts '84 P. 23)

ART. 4390b. No entire road of the first or second class shall hereafter be discontinued except upon vacation by order of the commissioners' court or non use for a period of three years.

Discontinu'ce of Road for non use

(Acts '84 P 24)

ART. 4390c. The report made by the supervisors of public roads to the commissioners' court, as provided for in article 4390a, shall be submitted, together with all contracts made by said court since its last report for any work on any road, to the grand jury, at the first term of the district court thereafter.

Supervisors report and contracts submitted to grand jury.
(Acts '84 P. 24)

9

ART. 4391. The commissioners' courts of the several counties shall lay off their respective counties into convenient road precincts, and shall number each precinct; and in the order establishing the same shall specify as definitely as practicable the boundaries thereof.

Co. Comm'ers shall lay off Road precincts.

ART. 4392. An overseer shall be appointed and hands apportioned by said court for each road precinct at the time of establishing the same; and at the first regular term of court in each year, the said court shall appoint an overseer for each road precinct in the county, and shall at the same time designate all the hands liable to work on public roads, and apportion them to the several overseers; *provided*, that hands shall as nearly as practicable be apportioned to work on the road precinct nearest to their place of abode; and *provided further*, that the supervisor of public roads shall at any time apportion any hands in his precinct who, from any cause, may not have been apportioned as otherwise provided in this act.

Appointm't of Road overseer.

Apportionment of hands.

ART. 4393. If from any cause the said court should fail to perform the duties required of it by the preceding article, at its first regular term in each year, it shall be competent and legal for said court to perform said duties at any subsequent term, whether the same be a regular or called term.

Can appoint other overseers at any term.

ART. 4394. In case of the death, removal or other inability act, of any road overseer, it shall be the duty of the county judge, immediately upon information of the fact, to appoint an overseer to fill such vacancy, who shall be notified of his appointment as in other cases.

In case of death, removal, &c. of overseer.

ART. 4395. It shall be the duty of the clerk of said court to make out copies of all orders appointing overseers of roads in duplicate, and deliver the same to the sheriff of the county within ten days after any such order shall have been made, endorsing on such copies the date of the orders of appointment.

Duty of clerk to make overseers' commissions

ART. 4396. All orders appointing overseers shall embrace the designation of hands liable to work under such overseer, as far as known, and shall specify the boundaries of such overseer's road precinct, as laid off by the court.

What it shall show.

ART. 4397. The sheriff shall, within twenty days after the reception of the copies of the orders appointing an overseer, deliver to, or leave at the usual place of abode of such overseer, one of such copies, and shall return the duplicate of such copy to the clerk of the county court, endorsing thereon the date and manner of service, and if not served the cause of his failure to serve the same.

Sheriff shall serve and make a return.

ART. 4398. The term of serivce of a road overseer shall be from the time of the service of the order of appointment until the first regular term of the commissioners' court in the succeeding year.

Term of service of Road overseer.

ART. 4399. No person shall be compelled to serve as an overseer who is lawfully exempt from road duty, nor shall any one be compelled to serve as overseer for more than one year in every three successive years.

Persons exm't as overseers.

ART. 4400. It shall be the duty of every person appointed overseer of a road, who is lawfully exempt from road duty, to notify the clerk of the county court of his non-acceptance, within ten days after his being notified of his appointment.

Duty of persons exempt to notify clerk.

ART. 4401 If any person appointed overseer of a road, who is lawfully exempt from road duty shall notify the clerk of his non-acceptance as provided in the

County Judge shall appoint another.

10

preceding article, the clerk shall forthwith report the same to the county judge, who shall immediately appoint another overseer for said road precinct.

ART. 4402. Should any person appointed overseer, and who is lawfully exempted from road duty, fail to notify the clerk of his non-acceptance within ten days after his being notified of his appointment, it shall be considered an acceptance of the appointment, and he shall not be permitted thereafter to plead his exemption from road duty as a defense against any neglect or failure to perform any of the duties of such overseer.

Failure to notify is an acceptance of appointment

ART. 4403. It shall be the duty of the clerk to insert on the copies of all orders or appointment of overseers issued by him, the duties required of overseers in regard to their non-acceptance of such appointment.

Clerk shall insert duties in regard to non-acceptance.

ART. 4404. The clerks of the county courts of the several counties in this State shall post up in their respective court houses, on the first day of each term of the district court held in his county, a list of the names and road precincts of all the overseers of roads in the county.

Clerk shall post list of overseers.

ART. 4405. All male persons between the ages of eighteen and forty-five years shall be liable, and it is hereby made their duty, to work on, repair and clean out the public roads under the provisions and regulations of this title, except ministers of the gospel in the active discharge of their ministerial duties, invalids, members of any company of volunteer guards organized under provisions of the title "Militia" and members of all volunteer fire companies in the active discharge of their duties as firemen, who shall be exempt. Amended March 24th, 1885.

Who are liable and who exempt from Road duty.

(Acts '85 P. 43)

ART. 4406. No person shall be compelled to work on a road who has not been residing in the county in which he is summoned to work for the space of fifteen days immediately preceding such summons.

Residence of fifteen days renders one liable to duty.

ART. 4407. Any person liable to road duty, and who has been summoned to do such duty, shall have the privilege to furnish an able bodied substitute to work in his place, which substitute shall be accepted by the overseer if he be capable of performing a reasonable amount of work; otherwise he shall not be accepted.

Substitute may be furnished.

ART. 4408. Every person liable to work on roads, by paying to his road overseer at any time before the day appointed to work on his road, the sum of one dollar for each day that he is summoned to work, shall be exempt from working for each day paid for, and also exempt from any penalties for failure to work for the time for which he has so paid.

Payment of money will release

ART. 4409. Each person summoned to work on a road shall take with him an axe, hoe, pick, spade or such tool as may be desired and directed by the overseer, or if he has no such tool as he is desired and directed by the overseer to take with him, he shall take such other suitable tool as he may have.

Hands shall bring tools.

ART. 4410. It shall be the duty of each road hand to perform his duties as such in accordance with the directions of his overseer, and a day's work, within the meaning of this act, shall be eight hours' efficient service, when said service is voluntarily performed.

Duty of hands to work eight hours.

(Acts '89 P. 21)

ART. 4411. No person shall be compelled to work on any public road or roads more than five days in each year.

Five days in one year.

(Acts '83 P. 23)

Road must be worked twice a year.

ART. 4412. Every overseer shall cause the road through his precinct to be worked at least twice in each year.

Power of overseers to call out hands.

(Acts '89 P. 2!)

ART. 4413. Overseers of roads shall have the power to call out all persons liable to work upon public roads at any time such overseer may deem it necessary, or when ordered by the commissioners' court or other competent authority, and such hands may be called out in detail, or the whole force at any one time, as may be deemed best, or as they may be directed, for the better improvement of the public roads.

Shall summon all persons liable to work

ART. 4414. In case any persons liable to work on roads shall not have been designated and apportioned by the commissioners' court, the overseer of the road nearest which such person lives shall summon such person to work on such road the same as if such person had been designated and apportioned to such overseer.

Mode of summoning hands.

ART. 4415. It shall be the duty of the overseer to give three days' previous notice, by summons in person or in writing, to each person within his road precinct liable to road duty in said precinct, of the time and place, when and where such person is required to appear to work on said road, and the number of days such person will be required to work.

Summons, how served.

ART. 4416. If the summons be in writing, it may be served by leaving the same at the usual place of abode of the person summoned, with some person residing at such place who is not less than ten years of age, or if no person ten years of age or over can be found at such place of abode, the overseer may serve the same by posting it on the door of such abode.

Overseer may appoint some one to summon hands.

ART. 4417. The overseer shall have power to appoint some one to summon the hands to work on the road, and such person shall be exempt from working on the road as many days as he was actually engaged in summoning the hands.

Overseer shall report defaulting hands.

ART. 4418. It shall be the duty of the overseer, within ten days after he has had his road worked, to file with the county attorney of his county, or the justice of the peace of his precinct, a complaint in writing and under oath, against any person who has been summoned to work and who has failed to work and failed to furnish a substitute, and has failed to pay one dollar for each day he has so failed to work or furnish a substitute, and also against each person so summoned who has refused to do a reasonable amount of work on the road, or who has refused to perform the reasonable directions of the overseer. The fact that the commissioners' court of the several counties will shortly meet and levy taxes for 1884, and the further fact that it is important for this act to go into effect immediately, for the purpose of securing to the people the full benefit of the recently adopted constitutional amendments, constitute an imperative public necessity, requiring that the constitutional requirment requiring bills to be read on three several days be suspended; therefore it is enacted that the constitutional rule be suspended, and that this act take effect from and after its passage.

Timber used to be paid for

ART. 4419. When to the overseer it may appear expedient to make causeways and build bridges, the timber most convenient therefor may be used; but in such case the owner of such timber shall be paid out of the county treasury a fair compensation for the same to be determined by the commissioners' court upon the application of such owner.

ART. 4420. The earth necessary to construct a causeway shall be taken from both sides, so as to make a drain on each side of such causeway.

Constructing drains.

ART. 4420a. Whenever it is necessary to drain the water from any public road, the overseer shall cut a ditch for that purpose, having due regard to the natural water flow, and with as little injury as possible to the adjacent land owner; provided, that in such cases the commissioners' court shall cause the damages to such premises to be assessed and paid out of the general revenues of the county, and in case of disagreement between the commissioners' court and such owner, the same may be settled by suit as in other cases.

Damages caused by drains.

Pay of.

(Acts '83 P. 80)

ART. 4421. When it may be necessary to use a wagon for any purpose in working a road, or a plow or scraper, the overseer of such road is authorized to exchange the labor of any hand or hands bound to work on such road, for the use of a wagon or wagons, plows or scrapers, and the necesary teams to operate the same, at reasonable rates, to be employed as aforesaid.

Overseer may exchange labor for team or wagon, &c.

ART. 4422. It shall be the duty of all overseers of roads to measure such parts of roads as are within their respective precincts in continuation, and set up posts of good lasting timber or stone at the end of each mile leading from the court house, or some other noted place, and to mark on said posts in legible and enduring figures the distance in miles to said court house or other noted place.

Road measured and mile posts.

ART. 4423. It shall also be the duty of overseers to place conspicuously and permanently, at the forks of all public roads in their respective precincts, and at all roads crossing or leading away from such public roads, index boards, with directions plainly marked thereon, stating the most noted place to which each of said roads leads.

Index boards.

ART. 4424. When a mile post or index board shall be removed or defaced by any means whatever, the overseer shall cause the same to be replaced immediately by another, marked as the original one.

Replace same when removed.

ART. 4425. The overseer is authorized to exchange the labor of any hand or hands bound to work on his road, for the making of index boards or mile posts, or either.

Exchange labor for mile posts.

ART. 4426. Overseers of roads shall apply all money coming into their hands as such overseers, to the improvement of their roads in an impartial manner, by repairing or building bridges, hiring hands or teams to work on the road, or in such other manner as he may deem best.

Overseer shall apply money, how.

ART. 4427. It shall be the duty of each overseer to report, in writing and under oath, to the commissioners' court of his county, at the first regular term thereof in each year, giving the number of hands and their names in the precinct liable to work on the roads; the number of days he has caused his road to be worked; the condition of such road; the amount of the funds received by him for his road; from whom received and for what purpose, and to whom and for what purpose said funds have been paid out, and the amount of such funds, if any, that remain in his hands; and he shall at the same time pay over to said court any such funds which may remain in his hands.

Overseer to report at the February Term.
(Use Barnard's form 1739; it saves labor to the overseer, the court and clerk.)

ART. 4428. Overseers shall retain out of money that may come to their hands as such overseers, ten per cent. thereof as compensation for their services, and during their term of service they shall be exempt from serving upon juries.

Ten per cent. to overseer and jury exemption.

ART. 4429. All moneys appropriated by law or by order of the commissioners' court for working public roads or building bridges shall be expended under the order of the commissioners' court, except when otherwise herein provided, and said court shall from time to time make the necessary orders for utilizing such money and for utilizing convict labor for such purpose.

Money to be spent under direction of Com'rs Court

ART. 4429a. Overseers shall dismiss from the road any hand or hands, whether working for themselves or as substitutes for others, who shall fail to do good and efficient work, or who shall hinder other hands from doing their work properly, or dismiss any hand who may be intoxicated, or who shall refuse to obey any reasonable order of the overseers; and the overseer shall proceed against such hand or hands so dismissed in the same manner as if they had refused to obey the summons to work upon the road.

Hands to be dismissed who fail to render efficient service or is drunk.

(Acts '89 P. 21)

ART. 4430. Overseers of roads shall cause bridges to be erected across all such water-courses and other places as may appear to them necessary and expedient; and should there be a water-course or other place that requires a bridge, dividing any two road precincts, the overseer of each of said precincts, together with their hands, shall meet at the same time and place to construct such bridge, and the overseer chosen by a majority of the hands present shall superintend the building of such bridge until finished.

Overseers shall have bridges built, when, &c.

(Act July 29, 1876, p. 67, §20)

ART. 3602. Any person who may be convicted of a misdemeanor or petty offense, and who shall be committed to jail in default of the payment of the fine and costs adjudged against him, may be worked upon the public roads or upon the county farms of the county in which such conviction is had, or be hired out to any individual, company or corporation within the county of conviction, to remain in said county, and the proceeds of said hiring, when collected, shall be applied, first, to the payment of the costs, and second to the payment of the fine; and every convict shall be entitled to a credit of twenty-five cents on his fine and costs for each day he may serve under such hiring, including Sunday, and he shall be discharged at any time upon payment of the balance due on his fine and costs or upon the expiration of his term of service, his term of service in no event to be greater than one day for each twenty-five cents of fine and costs: *Provided,* That in no case shall the counties be responsible to the officers for their costs, and in no case shall such convicts be hired out for a longer period than two years for failure to pay a fine and costs, and on the expiration of said time, unless by his hire such fine and costs have been sooner paid off, said convicts shall be finally discharged. Approved, March 1, 1887.

Co. Convict to be worked on road or Co. farm; officers' costs.

(Acts '87|P. 11)

CHAPTER III, ACTS 1889.

SECTION 1. *Be it enacted by the Legislature of the State of Texas:* That each county commissioners' court of this state may employ not exceeding four road commissioners for their respective counties, who shall be resident citizens of the district for which they are employed, and when more than one is employed, the district that each road commissioner is to control shall be defined and fixed by the court; such road commissioners when employed shall receive such compensation as may be agreed upon by the court, not to exceed two dollars per

Com'rs may employ four road commissioners, pay, $2 per day.

day for the time actually engaged. Each road commis- Give bond sioner, when employed, before he enters upon his duties, shall execute a bond, payable to the county judge of the county and his successors in office, in the sum of one thousand dollars, with one or more good and sufficient sureties, to be approved by the county judge, and conditioned for a faithful performance of his duties.

SEC. 2.—A road commissioner when employed shall Their powers. have control over all overseers, hands, tools, machinery and teams to be used on the roads in his district; and shall have the power to require overseers to order out his hands in any number he may designate for the purpose of opening, working, or repairing the roads or building or repairing bridges or culverts of his district; and it shall be the duty of such road commissioner to see that all the roads and bridges of his district are kept in good repair, and he shall, under the direction and control of the commissioners' court, inaugurate a system of grading and draining public roads in his district, and see that such system is carried out by the overseers and hands under his control, and shall obey all orders of the commissioners' court; and he shall be responsible Responsible for tools, &c. for the safe keeping and liable for the loss or destruction of all machinery, tools or teams placed under his control, unles such loss is without his fault, and [when] he shall be discharged he shall deliver them to the person designated by the court.

SEC. 3.—He shall expend such money as may be Shall expend money as directed by Com'rs Ct. placed in his hand by the commissioners' court under its direction in the most economical and advantageous manner on the public roads, bridges and culverts of his district; and all his acts shall be subject to the control, supervision, orders and approval of the commissioners' court; he shall work the convicts and such other labor as may be furnished him by the commissioners' court; and when the road commissioner shall have funds in his hands to expend for labor on the roads, and it shall be necessary for any overseer or overseers in his district to work more than five days during any one year upon the public roads, he may employ such overseers to continue their duties as such for such a length of time as may be necessary, and pay them for their services not more than one dollar and fifty cents per day for the time actually employed after the five days: *Provided,* That hands shall not be required to work when there shall be on hand, after building and repairing bridges, a sufficient road fund to provide for the necessary work on the roads.

SEC. 4.—Said road commissioner shall report to the Road Com'r to report to Com'rs each reg. term. commissioners' court at each regular term under oath, showing an itemized account of all money he has received to be expended on roads or bridges and what disposition he has made of the money, and showing the condition of all roads, bridges and culverts in his district, and such other facts as the court may desire information upon, and shall make such other reports and at such time as the court may desire.

SEC. 5.—Any road commissioner who shall willfully Penalty for failure to comply with this act. fail to comply with any of the provisions of this act shall be deemed guilty of a misdemeanor, and upon conviction shall be punished by fine of not less than twenty-five nor more than two hundred dollars.

SEC. 6.—The commissioners' court shall see that the Com'rs Court to see that money is judiciously spent. road and bridge fund of the county is judiciously and equitably expended on the roads and bridges of the county, and as nearly as the condition and necessity of the roads will permit, it shall be expended in each county commissioners' precinct in proportion to the amount collected in such precinct; and in expending money in building permanent roads the money shall first be used only on first or second class roads, and on those which shall have the right of way furnished free of cost to make as straight a road as is practicable to obtain and having the greatest bonus offered by the citizens of money, labor, or other property.

Certain roads to have preference.

SEC. 7.—The commissioners' courts are authorized to make all reasonable and necessary rules and orders for the working and repairing of public roads, and to utilize the labor to be used as money expended thereon, not in conflict with the laws of this state, and enforce such rules and orders; and they are further authorized to purchase or hire all necessary road machinery, tools or teams, and hire such labor as may be needed in addition to the labor not required of citizens to build or repair the roads.

Com'rs Court to make rules for working, to purchase tools, teams, etc.

SEC. 8.—Commissioners' courts or road commissioners may accept donations of money, lands, labor of men, teams, or tools, or any other kind of property or material to aid in building roads in their counties, and may authorize any person to make a drain along any public road for the purpose of draining his land, and require the person draining his land to do such work under the direction of the road commissioner.

Com's Court may accept donations to build roads and require certain work to be done under Road Com'r.

SEC. 9.—*Be it further enacted*, That this act shall not be construed to repeal any existing law, but it is cumulative and in aid of the existing law: *Provided*, That when road commissioners are employed the county commissioners are not required to supervise the roads as required by Article 4390a, Revised Statutes: *Provided*, Nothing in this law shall be construed so as to require more than five days' service in one year of any citizen.

When road Com'rs are app'nted Co. Com'rs not required to supervise road.

CITY AND TOWN.

SECTION 1. *Be it enacted by the Legislature of the State of Texas:* That in all cities and incorporated towns in the State of Texas in which from any cause their is not a de facto municipal government in the active discharge of their official duties, the commissioners' court of the county in which such city or incorporated town is situated shall assume and have control of the streets and alleys thereof, and shall have the same worked under the law and regulations for the working of public roads, and such streets and alleys for the purposes of this act shall be held and denominated public roads, provided, that all residents of any city or town, having no de facto city government, not otherwise exempt from road duty, shall be liable to road service as in other cases.

Cities and towns having no *de facto* government, Com'rs Court shall have control of streets.

(Acts '85 P.25)

ARTICLE 375. To have the exclusive control and power over the streets, alleys, and public grounds and highways of the city, and to abate and remove encroachments or obstructions thereon; to open, alter, widen, extend, establish, regulate, grade, clean and otherwise improve said streets; to put drains and sewers therein, and to prevent the encumbering thereof in any manner, and to protect the same from encroachment or injury; and to cause all able-bodied male inhabitants above 18 years of age, except ministers of the gospel, to work thereon not exceeding five days in any one year, or furnish a substitute or a sum of money (not to exceed one dollar for each day's work demanded) to employ said substitute, and to enforce the same by appropriate ordinances; and to regulate and alter the grade of premises, and to require the filling up and raising of the same; and such city council shall also have power to alter or vacate the alley in any block of ground within the city, upon the written application of the owner of the block, or if there

City Council to have power over streets, grounds and alleys.

May vacate an alley.

(Acts'89 P.1&2)

be more than one owner of such block, then upon the written application of all the owners thereof uniting in such application, and such alleys so vacated shall thereupon revert to and become the property of the owner of the block of which it was a part, or if more than one, then to the owners of the adjoining lots therein, each extending to the center of the alley so vacated.

SECTION 1.—*Be it enacted by the Legislature of the State of Texas:* That no public road shall be opened across lands owned and used or for actual use by the state, educational, eleemosynary, or other public state institutions for public purposes and not subject to sale under the general laws of the state, without the consent of the consent of the trustees of said institution and the approval of the governor of the state, and the roads heretofore opened across such lands may be closed by the authorities in charge of any such lands whenever they deem it necessary to protect the interests of the State, upon repayment to the county where the land is situated, with eight per cent. interest, the amount actually paid out by said county for the condemnation of said lands as shown by the records of the commissioners' court.

No road shall be opened across land owned by the State for educational and other purposes.

(Acts '89 P.134)

PENAL CODE.

OFFENSES PERTAINING TO PUBLIC ROADS AND IRRIGATION.

ARTICLE 408. If any person subject to public road duty under the laws of this State, shall willfully fail or refuse to serve as overseer of any road in his road district or precinct, when duly appointed as such overseer by the commissioners' court of his county, he shall be fined not less than ten nor more than fifty dollars.

Refusing to serve as overseer.

Penalty, $10 to $50.

ART. 409. If any overseer of a public road in this State shall willfully fail, neglect or refuse to perform any duty imposed upon him by law; or shall so fail, neglect or refuse to keep the road, bridges and causeways in his precinct or district clear of obstructions and in good order; or shall willfully suffer such road, bridges or causeways to remain uncleared and out of repair for twenty days at any one time, he shall be fined not less than ten nor more than twenty-five dollars.

Overseer failing to perform duty.

Penalty, $10 to $25.

ART. 410. If any overseer of a public road in this state shall fail, within six months of his appointment as such, to measure the road or roads in his precinct or district, and set up posts of lasting timber at the end of each mile leading from the court-house or some other noted place or town, and to mark on such posts, in legible words and figures, the distance in miles to said court-house or other noted place; or shall fail, when any such post is destroyed or removed, to replace the same with another marked as the original; or shall fail to affix or set up at the forks of all public roads in his district or precinct, index boards with directions pointing toward the most noted places to which they lead, he shall be fined in the sum of five dollars.

Overseer's failure to measure and set up posts, &c.

Penalty, $5.

ART. 411. If any person liable under the law to work upon the public roads shall willfully fail or refuse to attend, either in person or by substitute, at the time and place designated by the road overseer of his district or precinct, after being legally summoned; or shall fail, on or before the day for which he is summoned to attend, to pay to such overseer the sum of one dollar per day for each day he may have been notified to work on the road; or having attended, shall fail to perform any duty required of him by law and such overseer, he shall be fined in any sum not exceeding ten dollars.

Any person liable to road duty failing to attend or pay; penalty, $10.

17

ART. 412. Whenever the commissioners' court in any county in this state shall duly declare the boundary lines between the lands of different persons or owners a public highway, in accordance with law, if any such person or owner shall fail, neglect or refuse, for twelve months after legal notice thereof, to leave open his land free from all obstructions, for ten feet on his side of the line so designated, he shall be fined not more than twenty dollars for each month after the twelve months aforesaid, in which he may so fail, neglect or refuse.

ART. 413. Any person or persons placing a gate on or across any third-class road, or on or across any road such as is designated in article 412 of the penal code, shall be required to keep said gate and the approaches to the same in good order, and the gate shall be ten feet wide and so constructed as to cause no unnecessary delay to the traveling public in opening and shutting the same, and provide a fastening to hold said gate open till the passengers go through, and such person

or persons shall place a permanent hitching post and stile block on each side of and within sixty feet of such

gate. Any person or persons who may hereafter place a gate across a third-class road, or on or across any

road such as is designated in article 412, who shall willfully or negligently fail to comply with the requirements of this article, shall be deemed guilty of a misdemeanor, and on conviction may be fined in any sum not less than five dollars nor more than twenty dollars for each offense, and each week of such failure shall constitute a separate offense. Any person or persons who shall willfully or negligently leave open any gate on or across any third-class road, or on or across any road such as is designated in article 412, shall be deemed guilty of a misdemeanor, and on conviction may be fined in any sum as above provided for. Acts '84, p. 18.

GATEWAYS AND FENCES.

Unlawful to
fence over 3
lineal miles
in same general direction
without a
gate.
SECTION 1. *Be it enacted by the Legislature of the State of Texas:* That it shall be unlawful for any person or persons, by joining fences or otherwise, to build and maintain more than three miles, lineal measure, of fence running in the same general direction without a gateway in same, which gateway must be at least eight feet wide and shall not be locked. *Provided,* that all persons who have fences already constructed in violation of this section shall have six months within which to conform to the provisions.

SEC. 2. If any person or persons shall build or maintain more than three miles, lineal measure, of

fencing running in the same general direction, without providing such gateway, he shall be deemed guilty of a misdemeanor, and upon conviction shall be fined in any sum not less than one nor more than two hundred dollars, and each day that such fence remains without such gateway shall constitute and be punished as a separate offense.

SEC. 3. The provisions of this bill shall only apply to pasture land.

Com'rs shall
lay out one
first-class
road north
and south &
eastandwest
intersecting
at or near
center of
County.
SECTION 1. *Be it enacted by the Legislature of the State of Texas:* That the commissioners' courts of the several counties shall see that at least one firs-class road of the width prescribed by law, is laid out and opened from the county seats of their respective counties, on the most direct and practicable route, to the lines of their county, in the direction of the county seats of each adjacent county, where no part of another county intervenes between the county seats of such counties, or if a border county, to meet the nearest road to the

border, and if any adjacent county is not organized, then in the direction of the center of such county. And the commissioners' court of a county to which one or more unorganized counties are attached for judicial purposes, shall lay out and open at least two first-class roads, sixty feet in width, through the extent of each such unorganized county, to intersect at right angles as nearly as may be at the center of the county, and to meet at the county line similar roads of the adjacent counties. In the counties now having public roads substantially complying with the preceding requirement as to course, the court shall be required only to give such roads the width of sixty feet and clear them of obstructions; such roads, however, shall not be laid out across orchards, yards, lots or grave yards, or within one hundred feet of a residence without the consent of the owner; *provided*, that this law shall not apply to counties where there already exists a sufficiency of public roads.

Intended for unorganized attached counties chiefly.

Sec. 2. Provides that it shall be the duty of each commissioners' court within ninety days after the passage of this act, on their own motion, to appoint a jury of view to lay out the roads required in section 1, etc. As this act was approved Feb'y 7, 1884, and it contains no provision requiring counties thereafter organized to take similar action, and as the presumption is that the law has been complied with, we omit the latter portion of the act, which will be found in Acts '84, p. 63.

ROAD TAX

The acts of 1891, chap. 48 provides, that upon petition of 200 qualified voters, the commissioners' court may order an election to levy a tax not exceeding 15c. on the $100 worth of property, for road and bridge purposes.

Collin Co. has special road law. See acts '91. p. 66 and p. 154, sec. 26.

Lavaca Co. has special road law. See acts '91, p. 174.

GENERAL ROAD LAW

Authorizing Appointment of Road Superintendent.

The counties of Grayson, Travis, Houston, Dallas, Limestone, Fayette, Galveston, Cherokee, Gonzales, Wood, Raines, Harrison, Shelby, San Augustine, Sabine, Newton, Jasper, Tyler, Morris, Marion, Victoria, Goliad, Refugio, Aransas, Calhoun, Jackson, DeWitt, Hopkins, Comal, Upshur, Blanco, Camp, Gillespie, Lavaca, Parker, Panola, Milam, Lamar, Hill, Smith, Gregg, McLennan, Harris, Washington, Titus, Cass, Franklin, Delta, Angelina, Nacogdoches, Bowie, Montgomery, Walker, Trinity, Red River, Henderson, Van Zandt, Tarrant, and Jack counties are exempted from the provisions of this act. Provided, that the county commissioners' courts of Dallas and Collin counties may accept and adopt the provisions of this act, in lieu of the special acts for Dallas, Collin, Grayson and other counties, if in their judgment its provisions are better suited to Dallas and Collin Counties than the said special laws.

SECTION 1. *Be it enacted by the Legislature of the State of Texas:* That the commissioners' court of any county in this state may appoint one road superintendent for such county, or one superintendent in each commissioner's precinct, and such courts are authorized by an order made at any regular term thereof to determine

Com'rs' ct. may appoint one co. road superintendent for the co. or one for each com'rs' precinct.

whether there shall be one road superintendent for the county or one for each of the commissioner's precincts therein. Such order shall be entered on the minutes of such court and shall not be void for want of form, but a substantial compliance with the provisions of this act shall be sufficient. Provided no county shall be under the operations of this act whose commissioners' court does not appoint a road superintendent or superintendents as herein provided.

Com'rs' ct. to appoint one or four. SEC. 2. In case such commissioners' court shall determine that there shall be one "road superintendent," as provided in the preceding section, such court shall appoint a competent "road superintendent" for such county, and in case it is determined that there shall be four superintendents, then such court shall appoint a competent person as "road superintendent" for each commissioner's precinct in such county.

Shall give bond. SEC. 3. Each "road superintendent" whether county or precinct, shall, within twenty days after his appointment, take and subscribe the oath required by the constitution, and enter into bond payable to the county judge and his successors in office, with good and sufficient sureties to be approved by the county judge, in such sum as may be fixed by the commissioners' court, conditioned that he will faithfully do and perform all the duties required of him by law or the commissioners' court, and that he will pay out and disburse the funds subject to his control as the law provides, or the commissioners' court may direct, which bond shall be filed and recorded as other official bonds and shall not be void for the first recovery, but may be sued on from time to time until the full amount is exhausted.

Qualifications. SEC. 4. Every road superintendent shall be a qualified voter in the county or precinct, as the case may be, **Term of office.** for which he is appointed, and shall hold his office for two years or until his successor is appointed and qualified, but in all cases where the condition of the roads do not demand the continued services of the superintendent, his salary may, in the descretion of the commissioners' court, be suspended. The commissioners' court may for good cause remove any road superintendent, and in case of vacancy from any cause may appoint a successor who shall hold his office for the unexpired term.

Com'rs'ct. may remove.

Salary of Supt. SEC. 5. Each road superintendent shall receive such salary as may be fixed by the commissioners' court' to be paid on the order of said court at stated intervals, but the salary of the county superintendent, in counties of less than fifteen thousand inhabitants, shall never exceed one thousand dollars per annum; in counties of more than fifteen thousand inhabitants, it shall not exceed twelve hundred dollars per annum. That the salary of precinct superintendents in counties of less than fifteen thousand inhabitants shall not exceed three hundred dollars per annum, and in counties of over fifteen thousand inhabitants it shall never exceed four hundred dollars per annum.

Shall have supervision of roads. SEC. 6. The road superintendent, subject to the orders and directions of the commissioners' court, shall have the general supervision over all the public roads and highways of his county or precinct, as the case may be, and shall superintend the laying out of new roads, the making and changing of roads therein, the building of bridges therein (except where otherwise contracted), the working of the roads therein and all repairs to be made on the same, and over all county convicts worked on such roads, but this shall not prevent the commissioners' court from employing a person to watch and manage such convicts and direct the work to be done by them. Said road superintendent shall take charge of all tools, machinery implements and teams placed under his control by the commissioners' court and execute his receipt therefor, which shall be filed with the county clerk, and he shall be responsible for the safe keeping of all such machinery, tools, implements and teams, and the proper expenditure and paying out of all money belonging to the road fund that may come into his hands, and shall be liable for the loss, injury or destruction of any such tools, teams, implements or machinery unless such loss occurred without his fault, and for the wrongful or improper expenditure of any such money, and upon the expiration of his term of office, or in case of his resignation or removal, he shall deliver all such money and property to his successor or such other person as the commissioners' court may direct. Powers and duties. His responsibility.

SEC. 7. It shall be the duty of each road superintendent to see that all of the roads and bridges in his county or precinct, as the case may be, are kept in good repair, and he shall under the direction of the commissioners' court, inaugurate and carry out a system of working, grading and draining the public roads in his county or precinct, and shall see that every person subject to road duty in his county or precinct performs the work to which he is liable under the law. He shall act as supervisor of the roads in his county or precinct, as the case may be, and perform all the duties as supervisor that now devolves on the county commissioners under the existing laws in counties not adopting this act, and he shall do and perform such other service as may be required of him by the commissioners' court. Shall perform the duties now devolving on road supervisors.

SEC. 8. Each road superintendent in the counties where the commissioners' court so directs, as soon as practicable, shall divide his county or precinct, as the case may be, into road districts of convenient size, to be approved by the commissioners' court, and define the boundaries thereof and designate the same by number, which boundaries shall be recorded in the road minutes of the commissioners' court. And he shall ascertain the names of all persons subject to road duty in each road district, and keep a record thereof and report the same to the commissioners' court. Shall divide his co. into road districts. Report.

SEC. 9. Each road superintendent shall have power, and it shall be his duty to call out all persons liable to work on the public roads at any time and in such numbers as he may deem necessary to work the roads in their respective districts, and he shall utilize all such labor to the best advantage in connection with other labor on the roads. The call shall be summons served in the manner and for the length of time prescribed by the law regulating the calling out of hands by overseers, but no person shall be compelled to work outside of his road district. The road superintendent may appoint any person subject to road duty in any district to summon the hands to work the roads therein, and such person shall be exempt from road service as many days as he was actually engaged in summoning the hands, and in case of emergency he may appoint a deputy to supervise any particular work. He may also contract with any person subject to road duty, for the use of teams, and permit such person to discharge his road duty by the use of such double team; but he shall never allow more than two dollars per day for any team, nor more than three dollars for any hand and double team. Shall call out hands. May appoint some one to summon hands. Allowance for team.

21

SEC. 10. Each road superintendent shall make a report, under oath. to the commissioners' court, at each regular term thereof, showing an itemized account of all money belonging to the road fund he has received, from whom received, and what disposition he has made of the same, the condition of all roads and bridges in his county or precinct, as the case may be, and such other matters as the court may desire information upon; and shall make such other report at such times as such court may require.

SEC. 11. The commissioners' court of any such county is authorized to purchase or hire all necessary road machinery, tools, implements, teams and labor required to grade, drain or repair the roads of such county, and said court is authorized and empowered to make all reasonable and necessary rules, orders and regulations not in conflict with law, for laying out, working and otherwise improving the public roads, and to utilize the labor and money expended thereon and to enforce the same. But no change in any road shall be made that lengthens the same without it is to the benefit of the traveling public or for the protection of private property, and then only upon the unanimous consent of the commissioners' court.

SEC. 12. Each road superintendent shall employ sufficient force to enable him to do the necessary work in his county or precinct, as the case may be, having due regard for the condition of the county road and bridge fund and the quality and durability of the work to be done, and shall buy or hire such tools, teams, implements and machinery as the commissioners' court may direct, and he shall work such roads in such manner as the commissioner may direct, and such work shall at all times be subject to the general supervision of the commissioners' court.

SEC. 13. Each road superintendent shall make the best contract possible for all labor, tools, implements or machinery that he is authorized to hire or purchase, and in payment therefor he shall issue to the person entitled thereto his certificate showing the amount due and the purpose for which it was given, and upon approval by the commissioners' court a warrant shall shall issue therefor to the holder thereof on the county treasurer, to be paid by him out of the proper fund as other warrants. All such certificates shall be dated, numbered and signed by the road superintendent, and he and the sureties on his official bond shall be liable for all loss or damages caused by the wrongful issue of any such certificate or any extravagance in the amount thereof.

SEC. 14. The commissioners' court of any such county may, when deemed best, construct, grade, gravel or otherwise improve any road or bridge by contract. In such case the said court or the county judge may advertise, in such manner as said court may determine, for bids to do such work and the contract shall be awarded to the lowest responsible bidder, who shall enter into bond with good and sufficient sureties for the faithful compliance with such contract, but said court shall have the right to reject any and all bids. At the time of making any such contract the said court shall direct the county treasurer to pass the amount of money stipulated in such contract to a particular fund for that purpose, and the treasurer shall keep a separate account of such fund and the same shall not be used for any other purpose and can only be paid out on the order of said court.

22

SEC. 15. The commissioners' court may require all county convicts not otherwise employed to labor upon the public roads under such regulations as may be most expedient. Each county convict worked on the roads in satisfaction of any fine and costs shall receive a credit thereon of fifty cents for each day he may labor. And the commissioners' court may order that the county pay to the officers of court as much as one-half of the costs due them and adjudged against such convict, and upon such order such payment shall be made. But no such costs or any part thereof shall ever be paid until such convict has worked out the entire amount of such fine and costs as provided by law, and then only upon a certificate from such county or precinct superintendent to the effect that such costs have been so worked out. The commissioners' court may grant a reasonable commutation of time for which a convict would be compelled to work to pay his fine and costs, or for which he is committed, as a reward for faithful services and good behavior, and such court shall make proper rules and regulations under which such commutations may be granted.

SEC. 16. The commissioners' court may accept donations of money, lands, teams, tools, or labor, or any other kind of property or material to aid in building or keeping up roads in the county, and said court or any road superintendent, by and with the concurrence of the commissioners, may authorize any person to make a drain along any public road, the same to be done under the direction of the road superintendent, or such other person as such court may direct.

SEC. 17. The commissioners' court of any county may retain the system of working hands under overseers as provided by general laws, and place such overseers under the control of a county or precinct superintendent under such lawful regulations as said court may prescribe or may work with overseers without any superintendent, as may be deemed best.

SEC. 18. The commissioners' court of any county in which a special tax for the maintenance of the public roads is levied and collected, as provided for in section 9, article 8 of the constitution, shall not be compelled to require persons subject to road duty to work on the roads, as required in existing general laws, but in such counties the roads shall be worked wholly by taxation, or by taxation in connection with road service, as such court may deem best. In any such county such court may reduce the number of days that persons liable to road duty may be required to work on the roads, but can never increase the same above five days in any year.

SEC. 19. Each road superintendent shall keep an accurate account of all moneys received by him on account of the road or bridge fund, and pay the same over to the county treasurer within ten days after its collection, taking his receipt for the same.

SEC. 20. If any person liable under this act to work upon the public roads after being legally summoned, shall willfully fail or refuse to attend either in person or by able and competent substitute at the time and place designated by the person summoning him, or pay to the superintendent or other person authorized by the commissioners' court to receive the same, the sum of one dollar per day for each day he may have been notified to work on the road, or having attended, shall fail to perform good service or any other duty required of him by law, or the person under whom he may work, he shall be guilty of a misdemeanor, and on conviction thereof fined in any sum not less than five nor more than twenty-five dollars.

SEC. 21. Any road superintendent who shall willfully fail or refuse to comply with any provisions of this act or order of the commissioners' court shall be guilty of a misdemeanor, and on conviction thereof, punished by fine of not less than twenty-five nor more than two hundred dollars for each offense.

SEC. 22. Any person who shall knowingly or willfully destroy, injure or misplace any b.idge, culvert, drain, sewer, ditch, signboard, mile post or tile, or anything of like character, placed upon any road for the benefit of the same, shall be guilty of a misdemeanor, and upon conviction thereof, punished by fine of not more than five hundred dollars, and shall be liable to the county and any person injured for all damages caused thereby.

SEC. 23. The county superintendent or the precinct superintendent, as the case may be, shall obtain from the tax collector of their counties as soon after the first day of January of each year as practicable, and before the first day of May thereafter, a full list of the delinquent poll tax payers of such county for the previous year, and the persons so appearing on such list and who

are such delinquent poll tax payers shall be subject to road duty for the period of three days during such year, and they shall be summoned, as in other cases, to work the roads in the road district or precinct in which such person may reside, and the performance of the road service provided for in this section shall not exonerate the persons from any other road duty to which the persons performing the same may be subject, but this shall be taken as cumulative. The persons required to do road duty under the provisions of this section shall be subject to prosecution as provided in this act, or other law of this state, and subject to the same liabilities and punishments provided for in other cases for failing to appear or do good work, when summoned so to do, as provided for by this act or other law of this state, and all such laws shall apply to parties required to work under the provisions of this section. And when they are convicted for so failing to work the roads, shall satisfy the fine and costs as in other misdemeanor convictions. But any person summoned to work on the road under the provisions of this section may satisfy such summons and be relieved from such duty by, paying to the county road or precinct superintendent, as the case may be, three dollars; one-third of which sum shall go to the free school fund, and the balance to the road and bridge fund.

SEC. 24. The term "road" as used in this act includes road bed, ditches, drains, bridges, culverts, and every part of such road, and the terms "work" and "working" includes the opening and laying out of new roads, widening, constructing, draining, repairing, and everything else that may be done in and about any road.

SEC. 25. This act shall be cumulative of all other general laws on the subject of roads and bridges not in conflict herewith and where not otherwise provided herein such general laws shall apply; but in case of conflict with other general laws the provisions of this act shall govern.

24

SPECIAL ROAD LAW

For Grayson, Dallas, Galveston, Brown, Comanche, Mills,
Fannin, Travis, Hunt, Hill, Kaufman and Fayette
Counties, authorizing the employment
of a County Road Commissioner.

Passed March 5, 1891.

SECTION 1. *Be it enacted by the Legislature of the State of Texas:* That the commissioners' courts of Grayson, Dallas, Galveston, Brown, Comanche, Mills, Fannin, Travis, Hunt, Hill, Kaufman and Fayette Counties, if they deem it advisable so to do, may each employ one road commissioner for the county, who shall be a resident citizen of said county, and shall receive such compensation as may be fixed by said commissioners' court, not to exceed one hundred dollars per month, to be paid out of the road and bridge fund of said county. Said road commissioner shall be subject to removal at any time by the said commissioners' court. He shall, before entering upon the discharge of his duties, enter into a bond with two or more good and sufficient sureties, in the sum of $2000, payable to the county judge of the county and his successor in office, conditioned that such road commissioner will faithfully discharge the duties of his employment as such commissioner, which bond shall be approved by the county judge and acknowledged by the said commissioner and the sureties as required for the acknowledgment of deeds, and recorded as required for the bonds of county officers. *(margin: May employ a road commissioner. Shall receive such compensation as fixed by the com'rs ct. Shall give bond.)*

SEC. 2. Subject to the orders and control of the commissioners' court, the road commissioner shall have charge and control of all such teams, wagons, tools and machinery as the commissioners' court shall place in his custody for use on the public roads of said county and shall execute and deliver to the county clerk of said county his receipt therefor, specifying each item and its value, which shall be filed by the clerk of the county court in his office, and a certified copy thereof shall be admissible as evidence in any suit against said commissioner and his sureties or either of them, on his bond for the said property or the value thereof, the same as the original would be. Said road commissioner and his sureties shall be responsible on his bond for all such property thus turned over to him until he shall account therefor. *(margin: Subject to orders of com'rs' ct. Shall have custody of tools, etc. Responsible for same.)*

SEC. 3. The road commissioner shall have control of all road overseers in the county and shall deliver to each all teams, tools, wagons and machinery necessary in working the roads in the district of such overseers, so far as he has been supplied therewith by the commissioners' court, taking the receipt of said road overseer herefor, specifying each item and giving its value, which receipt shall be a full answer to the liability of the road commissioner for all such teams, wagons, tools, and machinery. It shall be the duty of the road overseer, when he has finished the work on his road, to return to said road commissioner all teams, wagons, tools and machinery received from him and to take up the receipt given for the same. *(margin: Shall have control of all road overseers. Take receipts for all tools, etc. from overseers, who shall return all when work is done.)*

SEC. 4. Each road commissioner and overseer shall, as to all teams, wagons, tools any machinery delivered to him by the commissioners' court or the road commissioner, be deemed and held to be the bailee of the county, and shall be responsible to the county for the value thereof until accounted for by him. It shall be *(margin: The com'r and overseers are bailees of the county and responsible for all property.)*

sufficient to exempt the road commissioner or any road overseer from liability for any property received by him as herein provided to show that he has delivered the same to any person authorized by law or by the orders of the commissioners' court of the county to receive the same, or that the same has died, been lost or destroyed without negligence or fault on his part.

Shall inform himself as to the condition of roads of the co.

SEC. 5. It shall be the duty of the road commissioner of the county, so far as practicable and as soon as possible, to inform himself of the condition of the public roads of his county, and under such rules and regulations as may be prescribed by the commissioners' court of said county, said road commissioner shall determine

Duties as to grade, etc.

what character of work shall be done upon the different roads of his county, and when and wherever needed, he shall establish the grade of such roads and direct the manner of draining the same, which directions shall be obeyed and observed by all road overseers unless changed by order of the commissioners' court.

Shall direct the calling out of hands and work.

SEC. 6. The road commissioner may require each road overseer to call out the hands under his direction in such numbers as may be sufficient to use the teams, wagons, tools and machinery allotted to such road district and at such times as may be necessary, but no road hand shall be required to serve in any one year exceed-

Overseers to have control of hands.

five days, unless the term of service as prescribed by the general law shall be extended beyond that term. Each road overseer shall have control of all hands within his road district and subject to road duty, and shall see that each said road hand shall perform his duty in work-ing said roads, and that each hand when called out shall

Shall see that they perform work.

perform a fair day's work, and if any hand so called out shall refuse to work in a proper manner, or to do his part of any service assigned to him, such road overseer shall treat him as if he had failed to appear in obedience to the summons, and such hand shall be liable to the same penalties as if he had failed to appear in obedi-

May be allowed pay for more than 5 days' work and may be exempted from duty one year.

ence to the summons. The commissioners' court may allow to any road overseer who shall be engaged in the active discharge of the duties of his office for more than five days during any one year, a compensation not to exceed $1.50 per day for the time so served over and above five days, and in addition thereto said court may enter an order exempting such road overseer from road duty in said county for the next succeeding year, if his service in the opinion of the court has been of a kind to merit such exemption.

Com'rs' ct. to have full power to systematize road work.

SEC. 7. The commissioners' court of said county shall have full power and authority to adopt such system for working, laying out and repairing the public roads in said county as to said court may seem best, and from time to time said court may change its plans or system of work in such manner as it may deem ad-visable. The said commissioners' court shall have the

May buy teams, tools, etc.

power to purchase such teams, wagons, tools and machinery as may be necessary for the working of its public roads and also all material that may be needed therefor, all of which shall be paid for out of the road and bridge fund of said county. The commissioners' court of the county may, in its discretion, work the county convicts of said county upon the public roads,

They may work co. convicts and commute time.

but it shall not pay any costs that may be adjudged against said convicts. As a reward for faithful services and good behavior while engaged at any work upon the public roads, the said commissioners' court shall have the authority to grant a reasonable commutation of time for which any convict would be compelled to work in order to pay his fine and costs, and such court shall make proper rules and regulations to govern and control in the granting of such commutation. The said commissioners' court shall have authority to employ such labor as may be necessary to work the public roads of the county, to be paid for out of the road and bridge fund; such labor shall be under the control of the road commissioner, if one shall be employed, or under such other person or persons as said court may direct and employ for that purpose.

SEC. 8. Every owner of a farm or other lands upon which a hedge of any description grows on or near the line of a public road shall be required to keep the same trimmed so that the height of the same shall not exceed five feet above the level of the ground, and any such owner who shall fail or neglect to so trim such hedge shall be notified in writing by the road overseer of that district to trim such hedge as herein required, and in case such owner shall, after receiving such notice, fail or refuse to so trim said hedge within a reasonable time, he shall be deemed guilty of a misdemeanor and upon conviction, shall be fined in any sum not to exceed $20 per week from and after the time that he received such notice, such fine to be paid into the county treasury and to be placed to the credit of the road and bridge fund of said county. If any owner of any farm shall fail or refuse after being notified as herein required to trim his hedge as required by this act, then the road overseer shall cause the same to be trimmed in accordance with the provisions of this act, to be paid for out of the road and bridge fund of the county.

SEC. 9. The commissioners' court of said county may make contracts for all supplies and materials to be used in feeding the hands and teams employed on the public roads and in the work of the same, and may make rules and regulations by which the same and all contracts shall be paid by the county, and all persons employed by said court shall be governed by such rules and regulations. The said court, may from time to time, make all necessary rules and regulations for the government of the road commissioner and all persons employed by said county on the public roads, which rules and regulations shall be entered upon the minutes of the court and a certified copy to be delivered to each person to be governed thereby. Said court may require of the road commissioner to make reports at such times and in such manner as may be prescribed by the said court, and any road commissioner refusing to make such reports shall be removed and shall be deemed guilty of a misdemeanor and upon conviction shall be fined in a sum not to exceed $100.00.

SEC. 10. Whenever it shall be necessary to occupy any lands, for the purpose of opening, widening, straightening or draining any road, or any part thereof, if the owner of such land and the county cannot agree upon the damages to be paid, the county may proceed to condemn the same in the same manner that a railroad company can condemn lands for right of way, and the same proceedings shall be had and the same rights shall exist as to each party as would exist if the proceedings were by a railroad company, except that the county shall not be required in any case to give bond.

SEC. 11. This act shall be taken notice of by all courts in the same manner as a general law of the state, and it shall be construed to be cumulative of all general laws of the state on the subject of roads and bridges where not in conflict therewith; but in case of such conflict this act shall control as to the said counties of Grayson, Dallas, Galveston, Brown, Comanche, Mills, Fannin, Travis, Hunt, Hill, Kaufman and Fayette. The term "roads," includes the roadbed, ditches and drains, the bridges and culverts, and every part of such road. The term "work and working" as used herein, shall include the opening and laying out of new roads, widening roads, constructing and building, repairing and draining of such roads, and everything that may be done in and about the maintenance of such road.

SEC. 12. The commissioners' court of each of the counties named in this act shall have the right to exercise all the authority and powers herein given, and neither of said counties shall be compelled to employ a road commissioner, unless the commissioners' court of such county shall deem it advisable so to do; provided, that the commissioners' court of either of the aforesaid counties shall appoint a road commissioner as herein provided for, then the county commissioners of the county, making said appointment shall not be required to perform the duties required of them by article 4390a of the revised civil statutes of the state.

)KEE, HOUSTON, ANDERSON,
ANKLIN, DELTA, HARRISON,
HUR, SHELBY, SMITH.

t enacted by the Legislature of the State What declared
l public roads and highways that public roads.
en laid out and established, agreea-
rokee, Houston, Anderson, Trinity,
Jpshur and Smith Counties, except
discontinued, are hereby declared to

mmissioners' courts of Cherokee, Co. com'rs ct.
l, Trinity, Franklin, Delta, Upshur, to open, lay out and dis-
Shelby and Smith counties shall have continue roads
hall be their duty, to order the lay-
g of public roads, when necessary,
or alter any road, whenever it shall
nt, as hereinater prescribed.

l be the duty of the commissioners' To classify
ll public roads in said counties into roads.
ird class roads.

ass roads shall be clear of all ob- First class
less than forty feet nor more than roads 40 to 60
l stumps over six inches in diameter ft., etc.
ix inches of the surface, and rounded
: inches and under to be cut smooth
nd all causeways made at least six-

class roads shall be clear of all ob- Second class
less than thirty feet wide. Stumps roads 30 ft., stumps cut
r in diameter to be cut down to six down, etc.
ce, and rounded off, and all stumps
l in diameter to be cut smooth with
useways to be made at least sixteen

lass roads shall be clear of all ob- Third class
less than twenty feet wide; stumps roads 20 ft.,
r in diameter to be cut down to six etc.
ce, and rounded off, and all stumps
l in diameter to be cut smooth with
iseways to be made at least sixteen

mlssioners' court shall in no instance Twenty days'
an application for any new road, or notice of new road or change
iginal one, unless the person making required.
r, or some one of them, shall have
ty days' notice, by written advertise-
nded application, posted up at the
: the county and at two other public
ty of the route of the proposed new
roposed to be discontinued.

ications for a new road, and all ap- Petition to be
ntinue an existing one, shall be by signed by ten
mmissioners' court, signed by at least freeholders.
the precinct or precincts in which
to be made or discontinued, specify-
a the beginning and termination of
. to be opened or discontinued.

s hereafter ordered to be made shall Jury of five to
y of freeholders of the county, to be lay out all
mmissioners' court. Said jury shall roads.
ions, a majority of whom may pro-
d mark the road so ordered, to the
: to the public, and with as little
ares as may be.

29

Oath of jurors.

SEC. 10. The jurors provided for in the preceding section shall, before proceeding to act as such, take th following oath before some officer authorized to admi ister oaths, to-wit: I,——, do solemnly swear that will lay out the road now directed to be laid out, by th order to us directed from the commissioners' court according to law, without favor or affection, malice o hatred, to the best of my skill and knowledge, so hel me God.

Jury to report.

SEC. 11. It shall be the duty of such jurors, whe qualified as provided in the preceding article, to pro ceed to lay out and mark the road, in accordance wit the order of the court and the law, and to report thei proceedings in writing to the next regular term of th commissioners' court.

Written consent of owner necessary.

SEC. 12. No public road shall be surveyed or lai out upon or across any farm, lot, or inclosure, withou first obtaining the written consent of the owner or hi agent or attorney to the same, except as hereinafte provided.

A jury to assess damages

SEC. 13. If such written consent shall be refused, i shall be the duty of the commissioners' court to ap point five disinterested freeholders, residents of th county, as commissioners, a majority of whom may act to view the same, assess the damages incidental to th opening of the road of the first, second, or third class through any part of said farm, lot, or inclosure, as pro posed, taking into consideration the advantages an disadvantages accruing to such owner from the opening of such road, and report their action in writing, an under oath, to the next regular term of the commissioners' court.

When owner protests same.

SEC. 14. If the owner of any inclosed land, his agent or attorney, shall file in the commissioners' cour a written protest against opening a road, viewed and marked out through such inclosed land, it shall be th duty of the commissioners' court to appoint five disinterested freeholders, residents of the county. as commissioners, a majority of whom may act, to view said road, assess the damages, and report in manner and form as provided in the preceding article.

Court may order road opened, first paying for land.

SEC. 15. If, in the judgment of the commissioners' court, from the report of the commissioners named in the two preceding sections, the road should be deemed of sufficient importance, the court may order the survey or opening of the same; but the court shall first order the payment of the damages assessed, if any, by the commissioners of view, to be made to the owner of the land, out of the county treasury, and the county treasurer shall have paid the same, or secured its payment, by a special deposit of the amount in his office, subject to the order of such owner, and shall notify such owner by mail or otherwise, of such deposit.

If no objection made.

SEC. 16. If no objection be filed, upon the report of a jury appointed upon an application to open a new road, the court shall proceed to establish and classify such road, and order the opening out of the same, and shall appoint an overseer and apportion hands for the same, as in other cases.

Com'rs may alter on application of one freeholder.

SEC. 17. The commissioners' court may alter or change the course of any public road, after notice, and upon application in the same manner as provided in this chapter for the discontinuance of a road, except that the application need not be signed by more than one freeholder of the precinct in which such alteration or change is proposed to be made.

30

SEC. 18. When juries of view are appointed, it shall be the duty of the clerk of the court to make out copies of the order appointing them, in duplicate, and to deliver such copies to the sheriff of the county within ten days after such order of appointment was made, indorsing on such copies the date of such order. Copies of order of appointment to be made.

SEC. 19. The sheriff receiving such copies shall serve the same upon the jurors by delivering to each of them, in person, a copy of the order of appointment provided for in the preceding article, or by leaving one of said copies at the usual place of abode of such juror. Service shall be made within twenty days after the sheriff receives said copies, and he shall make his return to the clerk on the duplicate copies, stating the date and manner of the service, or, if service has not been made, stating the cause of his failure to make the same. Sheriff to serve, manner of.

SEC. 20. Any juror of view, summoned as such, who shall fail or refuse to perform the service required of him by law as such juror, shall forfeit and pay for every such failure the sum of ten dollars, to be recovered by judgment, on motion of the district or county attorney, in the name of the county, in any court of competent jurisdiction in the county in which such defaulter may reside. Penalty of juror for failure to serve.

SEC. 21. For the further and better providing of public roads, any lines between different persons or owners of land may, upon the condition provided for in the following sections, be declared public highways and left open and free from all obstructions for ten feet on either side of said lines; but the marked trees and other objects used to designate said lines, and the corners of surveys, shall not be removed or defaced. Line roads.

SEC. 22. Whenever ten freeholders may desire the boundary lines between different persons or owners of land to be declared a public highway, in order to give them a nearer, better, or more practicable road to their church, county seat, mill, timber, or water, they may apply to the commissioners' court for an order establishing such road. How obtained.

SEC. 23. The application provided for in the preceding section shall be in writing, and shall be signed and sworn to by the applicants. It shall designate the lines sought to be opened, and the names and residences of the persons or owners to be affected by such proposed road, and shall state the facts which show the necessity for such road. Application in writing sworn to.

SEC. 24. Upon the filing of such application, the clerk shall issue a notice reciting the substance thereof, directed to the sheriff or any constable of the county, commanding him to summon the owners of the land, whose lines are proposed to be left open, naming them, to appear at the next regular term of the commissioners' court and show cause why said lines should not be declared public highways. Notice to owner.

SEC. 25. The notice provided for in the preceding section shall be served in the manner and for the length of time provided for the service of citation in civil actions in justices' courts, and shall be returned in like manner as such citations. How served.

SEC. 26. At a regular term of the court, after due service of notice, as provided in the preceding section, the commissioners' court may in its discretion, should it deem the road of sufficient public importance, issue an order declaring the lines designated in the applica- Com'rs may order road opened.

tion to be public highways, and direct that the same be opened by the owners thereof, and left open for the space of ten feet on each side of said lines.

Notice to owners. SEC. 27. When an order as provided in the preceding section is made, the clerk shall, without delay, issue a notice reciting said order or its substance, directed to the sheriff or any constable of the county, commanding him to serve the owners of such lines named in such notice with a true copy thereof, and the officer to whom How served by sheriff. said notice is delivered shall, without delay, serve the same as therein directed, and return the same to the clerk, indorsing thereon the manner and date of such service.

Not to be worked by road hands. SEC. 28. The commissioners' court shall not be required to keep any such road as is mentioned in the last seven sections, worked by road hands, as in case of other public roads.

Costs of neighborhood roads. SEC. 29. All costs attending the proceedings provided for in relation to opening neighborhood roads shall be paid by the applicants for any such road, whether their application be granted or not, and may be collected as other costs in civil action.

Com'rs may discontinue. SEC. 30. The commissioners' court may discontinue any neighborhood road which has been established as a public highway in the same manner provided in this act for discontinuing other public roads.

Right to erect gates. SEC. 31. The owner or owners of the land whose lines have been or may be declared public highways, and also any person through whose land a third class road may run, shall have the right to erect a gate or gates across said road or roads when necessary; said gate or gates to be not less than ten feet wide.

Damages, how assessed. SEC. 32. The amount of damages to be allowed to the owners of said lands for opening the lines of a neighborhood road, as provided in this act, shall be assessed as provided for in case of first, second and third class roads in this act. Said damages to be paid by the applicant or applicants for such road.

Road precincts numbered. SEC. 33. The commissioners' courts of Cherokee, Houston, Anderson, Trinity. Franklin, Delta, Upshur, and Smith counties shall lay off the counties into convenient road precincts, and shall number each precinct, and in the order establishing the same shall specify as definitely as practicable the boundaries thereof.

Appointment of road overseers. SEC. 34. An overseer shall be appointed by said courts for each road precinct at the time of establishing the same, and at the first regular term of the courts in each year the said courts shall appoint an overseer for each road precinct in the county, and shall at the same time designate all the hands liable to work on public roads and apportion them to the several overseers.

Same. SEC. 35. If from any cause the said courts should fail to perform the duties required of them by the preceding section, at its first regular term in each year, it shall be competent and legal for said court to perform said duties at any subsequent term, whether the same be a regular or called term.

In case of vacancy county judge to appoint successor. SEC. 36. In case of death, removal, or other inability to act of any road overseer, it shall be the duty of the county judges, immediately upon information of the fact, to appoint an overseer to fill such vacancy, who shall be notified of his appointment, as in other cases.

SEC. 37. It shall be the duty of the clerks of said ourts to make out copies of all orders appointing overseers of roads, in duplicate, and deliver the same to the heriff of the county within ten days after such order hall have been made, endorsing on such copies the .ate of the order of appointment.

SEC. 38. All orders appointing overseers shall embrace the designation of hands liable to work under uch overseer, as far as known, and shall specify the ioundaries of such overseer's road precinct as laid off iy the courts.

SEC. 39. The sheriff shall, within twenty days after he reception of the copies of any order appointing an iverseer, deliver to or leave at the usual place of abode of such overseer one of such copies, and shall return he duplicate of such copy to the clerk of the county iourt, endorsing thereon the date and manner of service, ind if not served, the cause of his failure to serve the iame.

SEC. 40. The term of service of a road overseer shall ie from the time of the service of the order of appointnent until the first regular term of the commissioners' iourts in the succeeding year.

SEC. 41. No person shall be compelled to serve as an iverseer who is lawfully exempt from road duty, nor shall any one be compelled to serve as overseer more :han one year in every three successive years.

SEC. 42. It shall be the duty of every person appointed overseer of a road, who is lawfully exempt from duty, to notify the clerks of the county courts of his non-acceptance within ten days after his being notified .of his appointment.

SEC. 43. If any person appointed overseer of a road, who is lawfully exempt from road duty, shall notify the clerks of his nonacceptance, as provided for in the preceding section, the clerk shall forthwith report the same to the county judge, who shall immediately appoint another overseer for said precinct.

SEC. 44. Should any person appointed overseer, and who is lawfully exempt from road duty, fail to notify the clerk of his non-acceptance within ten days after being notified of his appointment, it shall be considered an acceptance of the appointment, and he shall not be permitted thereafter to plead his exemption from road duty as a defense against any neglect or failure to perform any of the duties of such overseer.

SEC. 45. It shall be the duty of the clerks to insert on the copies of all orders of appointment of overseers issued by him, the duties required of overseers in regard to their non-acceptance of such appointment.

SEC. 46. The clerk of the county court shall post at the court house, on the first day of each term of the district court held in his county, a list of the names and the road precincts, of all the overseers of roads in the county.

SEC. 47. All male persons between twenty-one and forty-five years of age shall be liable, and it is hereby made their duty, to work on, repair, and clean out the public roads, under the provisions and regulations of this act, except ministers of the gospel actively engaged in the discharge of their ministerial duties, and invalids, and members of any company of voluntary guards organized under the provisions of the title "militia," who shall be exempt.

SEC. 48. No person shall be compelled to work on a road who has not been residing in the county in which he is summoned to work, for the space of fifteen days immediately preceding such summons.

SEC. 49. Any person liable to road duty, and who has been summoned to do such duty, shall have the privilege to furnish an able bodied substitute to work in his place, which substitute shall be accepted by the overseer if he is capable of performing a reasonable amount of work; otherwise he shall not be accepted.

SEC. 50. Every person liable to work on roads, by paying to his road overseer, at any time before the day appointed to work on his road, the sum of one dollar for each day that he is summoned to work, shall be exempt from working for each day paid for, and also exempt from any penalties for failure to work for the time for which he has so paid.

SEC. 51. Each person summoned to work on a road shall take with him an axe, hoe, pick, spade, or such tool as may be desired and directed by the overseer; or, if he have no such tool as he is desired and directed by the overseer to take with him, he shall take such other suitable tool as he may have.

SEC. 52. It shall be the duty of such road hand to perform his duties as such as required by law, and to do a reasonable amount of work, and in accordance with the directions of his overseer.

SEC. 53. No person shall be compelled to work on any public road or roads more than ten days in each year.

SEC. 54. Every insolvent poll tax payer, being a resident of the county, and not disqualified or excused by physical infirmity, who shall be indebted to the county on any unpaid county poll tax, and from whom the said poll tax cannot otherwise be collected by law, may be permitted to discharge the amount of such unpaid county poll tax in labor upon the public roads of his precinct, at the rate of one dollar per day; and in order to enforce the provisions of this section, the collector of taxes for the county shall be required on or before the second Monday in May of each year, to furnish to the several overseers of the counties, the names of all the defaulting poll tax payers, together with the amount of county poll tax due and unpaid by each, for which ex-officio service the collector shall be exempt from road duty five days; and it shall be the duty of the overseer, whenever any such person shall have discharged his county poll tax as herein provided, to report the same in his regular reports to the commissioners' courts. *Provided*, that no penalty shall ever be imposed upon poll tax payers for refusal or failure to work upon the public roads.

SEC. 55. This act shall be cumulative of all laws of the State on the subject of roads and bridges and employment of county convicts not in conflict herewith, and where not otherwise provided herein such general laws shall apply; but in case of conflict with general laws, this act shall govern; and the courts of the State shall have and take judicial cognizance of this act in the same manner and to the same extent as they are required to know and notice the general laws of the State.

Approved April 19, A. D. 1893.

ROADS — CAMERON, HARRIS, FAYETTE, DAL-
LAS, BRAZOS, CORYELL, BEXAR, ROCKWALL
AND ELLIS COUNTIES.

SECTION 1. *Be it enacted by the Legislature of the State* May construct
of Texas: That the county commissioners' courts of permanent
Cameron, Harris, Fayette, Dallas, Rockwall, Brazos, roads.
Coryell, Bexar and Ellis counties, State of Texas, may,
as hereinafter provided, build or construct, or cause to
be built or constructed, in said counties, lasting or permanent county roads and bridges, of some permanent
or durable material, to be selected and agreed upon by
said commissioners' courts, and may also construct
drains or ditches to carry off the water from such road
or roads, and from lands adjacent thereto, whenever
and wherever same can be done without conflicting with
the rights of private property owners, and may take May acquire
and condemn any land or lands necessary for the pur- necessary
pose of constructing roads or drains under its general land.
powers of eminent domain.

SEC. 2. Whenever the commissioners' courts of said May issue
counties shall deem it necessary or expedient to build bonds for
or construct any public roads and bridges of the char- bridges if rati-
acter herein provided for, they shall pass a resolution, electors.
which may be done at any regular or special meeting
of said courts, setting forth that it is the sense of said
commissioners' court that public roads and bridges of a
lasting or permanent nature should be constructed or
built in said county, and that the county should issue
its bonds to raise money for that purpose. Said resolution shall be submitted to a vote of the property owners
of said counties at any regular or special election, which
may be ordered by the commissioners' court for that
purpose; and if at such election, a majority of the votes
cast shall be for said resolution, the same shall be
adopted; but if a majority of votes cast at such election shall be against said resolution, it shall be rejected.
Such election shall be governed in all respects by the
laws governing elections in this State, and the returns Manner of
shall be made and canvassed in the same manner, and election.
the result declared by proclamation of the county judge,
which proclamation shall be posted in at least three
public places in said counties, and at the option of the
commissioners' court published in some newspaper in
said counties.

SEC. 3. No person shall be permitted to vote at any Qualifications
election, as provided for in section 2 of this article, un- of electors.
less he is a property owner and taxpayer in said coun-
ties of Harris, Fayette, Cameron, Dallas, Rockwall,
Brazos, Coryell, Bexar or Ellis, and unless he is otherwise a qualified voter of said county. Those desiring
to vote for the resolution shall have written or printed
on their tickets the words, " For the resolution to issue
bonds to build permanent county roads and bridges,"
and those desiring to vote against the resolution shall
have written or printed on their tickets the words,
' Against the resolution to issue bonds to build per- Manner of
manent county roads and bridges." Such tickets shall voting.
be written or printed on plain white paper with black
ink, and shall contain no distinguishing mark or de-
vice, except the words above set out, and if printed,
shall be in type of uniform size and face.

SEC. 4. If, at the election herein provided for, a Com'rs to can-
majority of the qualified voters at such an election shall vass vote.
vote in favor of the resolution provided for in section 2
of the act, and after the commissioners' court has canvassed the said vote and declared the result, and after

35

the proclamation of the county judge declaring said result has been posted for at least thirty days, it shall be the duty of the county commissioners' court, under the supervision and direction of the Comptroller of this State, to prepare and execute the bonds of the county for such sums as may be deemed advisable by said commissioners' courts, said bonds to bear not exceeding five per cent. interest, payable annually, and which shall be redeemable in not less than ten years and not more than forty years from the date thereof, the maturity to be expressed on the face of the bonds, and shall have the same registered or enrolled, as in the case of other county bonds, and the same shall not be sold or negotiated at less than their face or par value: *Provided*, that in no case shall said county issue bonds under this act for a greater sum or amount than a levy of fifteen cents on the hundred dollars property valuation of such county will yield sufficient revenue to pay the interest as it accrues, and will at the same time create a sinking fund sufficient to pay the principal at maturity.

Bonds to bear 5 per cent. interest redeemable in ten years.

SEC. 5. When the bonds of the county are issued and sold under the provisions of this act, it shall be the duty of the county commissioners' court of said county to levy an annual ad valorem tax on all property of the county, which tax, when collected, shall be used only for the purpose of paying the interest on the county road and bridge bonds, and create a sinking fund to pay the principal of same; and after the adoption of the resolution as herein provided for, it shall be unlawful for the county commissioners' court to transfer any funds from the road and bridge fund to any other fund of said county, or to divert the funds arising from the sale of such bonds, or any funds that may be derived from the road and bridge tax of said county to any other purpose than the construction and maintenance of county roads and bridges. Should the commissioners' court of said counties divert any funds contrary to the provisions of this act, they and each member of said court so acting or voting shall be deemed guilty of malfeasance in office, and on conviction shall be punished by a fine of two hundred dollars, and may be removed from office.

Tax to be levied to pay bonds.

Cannot divert fund.

SEC. 6. Whenever there shall be or remain in the treasury of this State any moneys to the credit of the permanent school fund, uninvested, the State Board of Education is authorized and empowered to lend the same to said county, when it shall have complied with the foregoing provisions of this act, by purchasing at par value the permanent road and bridge bonds of said county, when satisfactory evidence is presented to said board that all the provisions of this act have been complied with. And the State Board of Education shall have the preference to purchase said permanent road and bridge bonds, when there is sufficient permanent school funds in the treasury, and they are satisfied that all requirements of law in reference to the issuing of said bonds have been complied with. Should there not be sufficient money in the treasury to the credit of the permanent school funds to purchase the whole issue of such county road and bridge bonds, then the State Board of Education may purchase said bonds to the extent of the funds on hand, or the county commissioners' court may, at their option, place said issue of bonds elsewhere, as to them may seem best for the interest of the county, and in like manner, the county permanent school fund may be invested in such county bonds, and whenever said county shall have on hand permanent school funds uninvested, said county shall have the

State Board of Education may purchase the bonds.

preference to invest said funds in the road and bridge bonds of said county.

SEC. 7. The moneys arising from the sale of the bonds herein provided for shall not be used for any other purpose than for the construction of durable and permanent county roads and bridges, and the purchase of material therefor, and any county commissioners' court, or any county commissioner, or any other person, who shall misapply or convert same or any part thereof, to any other purpose than the one named, shall be deemed guilty of malfeasance in office, and on conviction shall be punished as hereinbefore provided for that offense. *Funds realized cannot be diverted,*

SEC. 8. All roads and bridges built under the provisions of this act shall be laid out and constructed under the supervision of the county commissioners' court, and a competent civil engineer, the county surveyor, or other competent person, to be employed by the county for that purpose. *Road to be constructed under supervision of co. com'rs and civ. engineer.*

SEC. 9. That all laws and parts of laws in conflict with the provisions of this act be and the same are hereby repealed.

ROADS — COLLIN, GRAYSON, WILLIAMSON, LAMAR AND BELL COUNTIES.

SECTION 1. *Be it enacted by the Legislature of the State of Texas:* That each member of the commissioners' court of Collin, Grayson, Williamson, Lamar and Bell counties shall be ex-officio road commissioner of their respective districts, and under the direction of the commissioners' court shall have charge of all the teams, tools and machinery belonging to the county, and placed in their hands by said court; and it shall be their duty, under such rules and regulations as the commissioners' court may prescribe, to superintend the laying out of new roads, the making or changing of roads, and the building of bridges. Each of said commissioners shall, before entering upon the duties of their office, execute a bond of one thousand dollars, with two or more good and sufficient sureties, payable to the county judge of said county for the use and benefit of the road and bridge fund, conditioned that they will perform all the duties required of them by law or by the commissioners' court, and that they will account for all money or property belonging to the county that may come into their possession: *Provided,* that with the consent of the commissioners' court any one of said commissioners shall be allowed to appoint any competent person as deputy road commissioner, who shall be required to execute the same bond that is required of commissioners in this section; and such deputy road commissioners shall be entitled to the same compensation that is allowed county commissioners for the same service: *Provided,* that county commissioners shall not be allowed any compensation as road commissioners when a deputy road commissioner has been appointed. *Co. com'rs ex-officio road com'rs.* *Shall give bonds.* *May appoint a deputy.*

SEC. 2. The commissioners' court of said counties shall have full power and authority, and it shall be their duty, to adopt such system for working, laying out, draining, and repairing the public roads in said counties as they may deem best, and from time to time said court may change its plans or system of working. Said commissioners' court shall have power to purchase *Power of com'rs court.*

37

May let contract to work road.

such teams, tools and machinery as may be necessary for the working of its roads. Said court shall have the power to construct, grade, or otherwise improve any road or bridge by contract. In such case said court, or the county judge, may advertise, in such manner as said court may determine for bids to do such work, and the contract shall be awarded to the lowest responsible bidder who shall enter into bond, payable to the county judge of said county, for the use of the road and bridge fund, with good, sufficient sureties, to be approved by said court, and in such sum as said court may determine, for the faithful compliance with the terms of said contract, but said court shall have the right to reject any and all bids. At the time of making any such contract the court shall direct the county treasurer to pass the amount to a particular fund for that purpose, and the treasurer shall keep a separate account of such fund, and the same shall not be used for any other purpose, and can only be paid out on the order of said court; and the said court shall have the authority to employ any hands or teams to work on the roads, under such regulations and for such price as they may deem best.

Co. treas. to keep separate accounts.

Co. convicts to work road.

Sec. 3. The commissioners' court of said counties shall require all county convicts not otherwise employed, to labor upon the public roads, under such regulations as it may prescribe, and each convict so worked shall receive a credit of fifty cents on his fine first, and then on the cost, for each day he may labor. The commissioners' court may, at a regular term, allow to the officers and witnesses such amount of their cost for the arrest and conviction of said convict as it may deem best: *Provided*, that it shall not allow to any officer an amount greater than the following: County judge, $3.00; county attorney, $5.00, including commissions; county clerks and justices of the peace, $1.70: sheriffs or constables, $2.00; which amount shall be paid to the officers out of the road and bridge fund, on the warrant of the county judge, when said fine and costs shall have been worked out as provided in this section: *Provided*, that this shall not be construed as to relieve any convict from the payment of all costs for which he would be liable under the general laws of this State. The commissioners' court may grant a reasonable commutation of time for which a convict is committed as a reward for faithful service and good behavior: *Provided*, that such commutation shall in no case exceed one-tenth of the whole time. The commissioners' court may provide the necessary houses, prisons, clothing, bedding, food, medicine, medical attention, and guards, for the safe and humane keeping of convicts.

Co. officers' costs.

May grant commutation of time.

Prisoners' food, guards, medicine, etc.

Co. com'r to have control of all road overseers.

Sec. 4. Each county commissioner shall have control of all road overseers in his district, and shall deliver to each of them all teams, tools and machinery necessary in working the roads in the district of said overseer, so far as he has been supplied therewith by the commissioners' court, taking receipt of said road overseer therefor, specifying each item and giving its value, which receipt shall be a full answer of the liability of the commissioner, and shall fix the liability of the overseer; and any commissioner or overseer who shall have been entrusted with any team, tools or machinery belonging to said county, shall be liable for any damage that may occur to the same while in his possession. It shall be the duty of the road overseer, when he has finished work on his road, to return to said commissioner all teams, tools and machinery received from him, and to take up the receipt given therefor.

Return of all teams, tools etc.

Sec. 5. It shall be the duty of the county commissioner, when acting as road commissioner, to inform himself of the condition of the public roads in his district, and shall determine what character of work shall be done upon said roads, and shall direct the manner of grading, draining, or otherwise improving the same, which directions shall be observed and obeyed by all road overseers of his district.

Supervision of work by road com'r.

SEC. 6. The commissioners may require each road overseer in his district to call out the hands in such numbers as may be sufficient to perform the work, but no road hand shall be required to work exceeding five days in any one year, unless the term of service as prescribed by the general laws shall be extended beyond that time: *And provided*, that all road hands in a particular district shall, as far as practicable, be worked a uniform time. Each road overseer shall have full control of all road hands within his road district, and he shall see that each hand, when called out, shall perform a good day's work; and if any hand, when so called out, shall fail or refuse to perform a good day's work, or to work in the manner the overseer may direct, he shall be liable to the same penalty as if he had failed to appear in obedience to the summons. The commissioners' court may allow to any overseer who may be engaged in the discharge of the duties of his office for more than five days during any one year, a compensation, not to exceed one dollar and one-half per day, for the time so served.

Road hands may work five days a year.

Hands shall work, penalty for failure.

Extra time of overseer.

SEC. 7. Any citizen of Collin, Grayson, Lamar, Williamson and Bell counties, liable for road duty, and who shall, on or before the first day of January of any year, pay to the county treasurer the sum of $3.00, shall be exempt from road duty for such year, beginning on the first day of January. The treasurer shall receive and receipt for all money so paid him, and place the same to the credit of the road and bridge fund, and he shall keep a separate account for each road district from which it is received. The treasurer shall, on the third day of January, or as soon thereafter as practicable, furnish to each county commissioner a list of all persons in their respective districts that have paid said sums as provided in this section.

Payment of $3 before Jan. 1st. exempts.

Duty of co. treas., report, etc.

SEC. 8. Whenever it shall be necessary to occupy any land for the purpose of opening, widening, straightening or draining any road or part thereof, if the owner of such land and the county commissioners' court cannot agree upon the damage to be paid, the county may proceed to condemn the same in the same manner that a railway company can condemn land for right of way, and the same proceedings may be had, and the same rights shall exist to each party as would exist if the proceedings were by a railroad company, except that the county shall in no case be required to give bond.

May condemn land.

SEC. 9. Every owner of a farm or other lands, upon which a hedge of any description grows on or near the public road, shall be required to keep the same trimmed so that the height of the same shall not exceed eight feet above the level of the ground. Any such owner who shall fail or neglect to so trim such hedge, shall be notified in writing by the road overseer of that district to trim such hedge as herein required; and in such case [if] such owner shall, after receiving such notice, fail or refuse to so trim such hedge within a reasonable time, he shall be deemed guilty of a misdemeanor, and upon conviction shall be fined in any sum not to exceed $20.00 per week from and after the time he received such notice; such fine to be paid into the county treasury and to be placed to the credit of the road and

Hedges to be trimmed, etc.

Penalty for failure.

bridge fund of said county. If any owner of any farm shall fail or refuse, after being notified as herein required, to trim his hedge as required by this act, then the road overseer shall cause the same to be trimmed in accordance with the provisions of this act, to be paid out of the road and bridge fund of the county.

Pay of road com'r.

SEC. 10. Each county commissioner, when acting as road commissioner, and performing the duties imposed upon him by law, or by the commissioners' court, shall be entitled to two dollars per day for the services actually performed: *Provided*, that he shall not receive more than forty-five dollars ($45.00) per quarter, when the road and bridge tax has not been levied as provided by law, under the amendment of 1889, as adopted in 1890, to the Constitution of the State of Texas. And when said tax shall have been levied he may receive an amount not to exceed ninety dollars ($90.00) per quarter, which amount shall be paid out of the road and bridge fund, when the account shall have been approved by the commissioners' court, and the court shall not approve said account unless the commissioner presenting it shall sign an oath that the account is just, due and unpaid, and specifying the number of days' work actually performed by him, and that it was necessary to be done; and no commissioner shall be entitled to pay as road commissioner while he is performing the duties of a county commissioner.

Account rendered under oath.

SEC. 11. This act shall be taken notice of by all courts in the same manner as the general laws of the State, and it shall be construed to be cumulative of all general laws of the State on the subject of roads and bridges when not in conflict therewith; but in a case of conflict this act shall control as to the counties of Collin, Grayson, Williamson, Lamar and Bell; and an act passed at the regular session of the Twenty-second Legislature, approved April 4, 1891, providing a special road law for Collin county, is hereby repealed.

40

The number of hands liable to work the roads in this Precinct, and their names, are as follows:

1 ....
2 ....
3 ....
4 ....
5 ....
6 ....
7 ....
8 ....
9 ....
10 ....
11 ....
12 ....

26 ....
27 ....
28 ....
29 ....
30 ....
31 ....
32 ....
33 ....
34 ....
35 ....
36 ....
37 ....

38
39
40
41
42
43
44
45
46
47
48
49
50

13
14
15
16
17
18
19
20
21
22
23
24
25

The number of hands liable to work the roads in this Precinct, and their names—Continued.

51 ....   76 ....

52 ....   77 ....

53 ....   78 ....

54 ....   79 ....

55 ....   80 ....

56 ....   81 ....

57 ....   82 ....

58 ....   83 ....

59 ....   84 ....

60 ....   85 ....

61 ....   86 ....

62 ....   87 ....

88

89

90

91

92

93

94

95

96

97

98

99

100

63

64

65

66

67

68

69

70

71

72

73

74

75

The total amount of money collected in fines and otherwise, under the provisions of the law, is .... DOLLARS, received from the following named persons:

FROM		FROM	
		Amount of Commission at 10 per cent	
		Total	

Amount paid out under the law is as follows, viz :

To................................, For...

To................................, For...

To................................, For...

To................................, For...

To................................, For...

To................................, For...

To................................, For...

To................................, For...

To................................, For...

To................................, For...

Total................

Balance due.

List of Property on hand at time of Appointment.

_____

Memorandum of Implements Purchased.

_____

www.ingramcontent.com/pod-product-compliance
Lightning Source LLC
Chambersburg PA
CBHW021552270326
41931CB00009B/1182